11/24/15
CPI
17.70

.8

Spotlight on the 13 Colonies
Birth of a Nation

THE COLONY OF
NEW YORK

Greg Roza

PowerKiDS press™

New York

Published in 2016 by The Rosen Publishing Group, Inc.
29 East 21st Street, New York, NY 10010

Editor: Katie Kawa
Book Design: Andrea Davison-Bartolotta

Library of Congress Cataloging-in-Publication Data

Roza, Greg.
The colony of New York / by Greg Roza.
p. cm. — (Spotlight on the 13 colonies: Birth of a nation)
Includes index.
ISBN 978-1-4994-0537-8 (pbk.)
ISBN 978-1-4994-0541-5 (6 pack)
ISBN 978-1-4994-0544-6 (library binding)
1. New York (State) — History — Colonial period, ca. 1600 - 1775 — Juvenile literature. 2. New York (State) — History — 1775 - 1865 — Juvenile literature. I. Roza, Greg. II. Title.
F122.R69 2015
974.7'02—d23

Manufactured in the United States of America

CPSIA Compliance Information: Batch #WS15PK: For further information contact Rosen Publishing, New York, New York at 1-800-237-9932.

Contents

Before It Was New York

For hundreds of years before Europeans "discovered" what they called the **New World**, it had been home to many Native American groups. The Iroquois nations and Algonquian-speaking peoples were the two main groups living in the area today called New York when the first Europeans arrived.

In 1524, Italian explorer Giovanni da Verrazano was the first European to visit New York. He sailed into present-day New York Harbor looking for a water route through North America to Asia. At that time, ships traveled around South America to reach Asia. When Verrazano didn't find a new route, he returned to Europe.

In 1609, the Englishman Henry Hudson arrived in New York and sailed up the river that was later named for him. Hudson had been hired by the Netherlands' Dutch East India Company to find a water route to Asia. Hudson didn't find a route to Asia, but he did claim a large area of land in New York for the Netherlands. He called this land New Netherland.

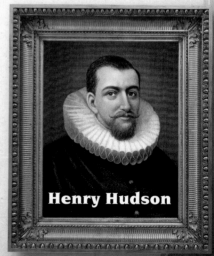

Henry Hudson

Giovanni da Verrazano was born in Italy, but he was sent by King Francis I of France to find a water route to Asia.

J.W. ORR NY

The Dutch West India Company

Dutch merchants in the Netherlands wanted to make money by trading for North American furs. They formed the Dutch West India Company in 1621 and set up trading posts in North America. Soon after, Dutch ships traveled to New Netherland to trade with the Native Americans who lived there.

In 1624, people from the Netherlands and other European counties started settling in New Netherland. That year, Fort Orange—near what is now Albany, New York—was established as a trading post. Many of the colonists were French-speaking Protestants named Walloons. The Dutch West India Company encouraged Protestants to go to New York by telling them they could practice their religion freely.

The Dutch West India Company drew more settlers to New Netherland by offering large areas of land to people who were known as **patroons**. Patroons paid for settlers to travel to New Netherland and farm their land. African slaves were also forced to farm the land.

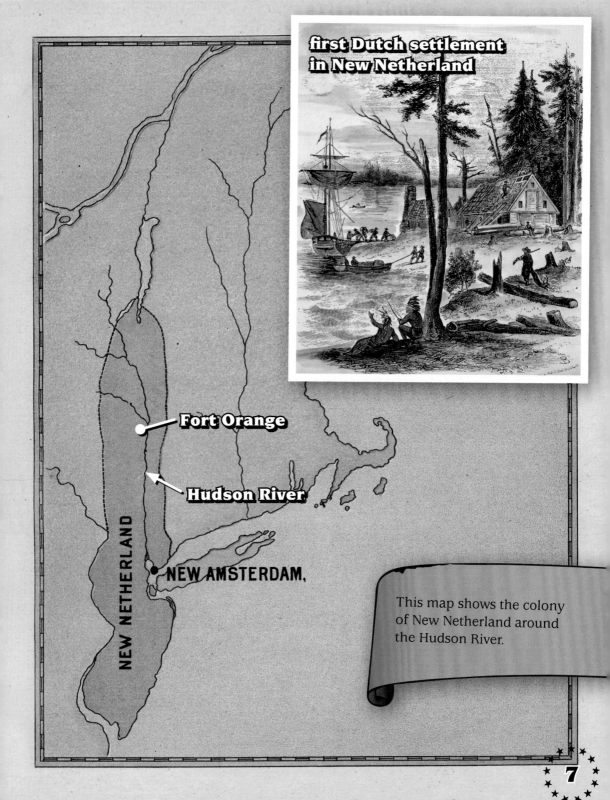

first Dutch settlement in New Netherland

Fort Orange

Hudson River

NEW NETHERLAND

NEW AMSTERDAM,

This map shows the colony of New Netherland around the Hudson River.

Founding New Amsterdam

In 1626, the Dutch West India Company purchased Manhattan Island from local Native Americans and established the colony of New Amsterdam. The colony was named after Amsterdam, which is a city in the Netherlands. The colonists built a wall at one end of the settlement to keep it safe. The place where the wall was located is today's Wall Street.

During the late 1620s, New Amsterdam grew quickly. Its harbors on the Atlantic Ocean and the Hudson River drew trading ships from all over the world. In 1626, Dutch ships brought the first African slaves to New Amsterdam.

In 1638, the Dutch government sent Willem Kieft to lead the colony and increase profits. Kieft tried to tax Native Americans, which led to a war. After colonists won the war, Kieft was removed from office. In 1647, Petrus (Peter) Stuyvesant became the governor of New Amsterdam. The colonists found him to be a stern leader, but he worked hard to make New Amsterdam a better place.

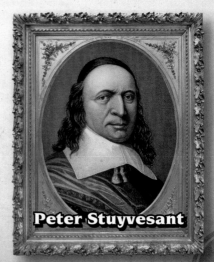
Peter Stuyvesant

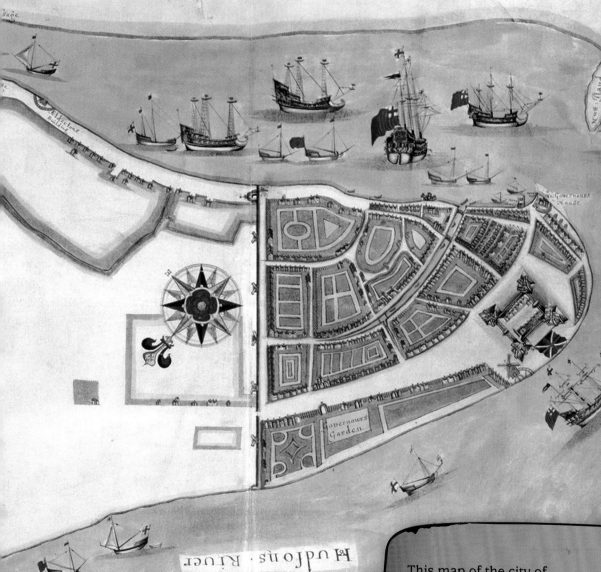

LONGE · ISLELAND ·

Hudfons · Riuer

THE · MAINE · LAND

This map of the city of New Amsterdam was created in 1664.

England Takes Over

In the early 1660s, England had colonies to the north and south of New Netherland. They had also claimed land in Connecticut and Long Island, which the Dutch had claimed as well. In 1660, Charles II became the king of England. He wanted to unify the English colonies in North America in order to increase his control of the land's resources. He also wanted to break the control the Netherlands had on trade in the area.

In 1664, Charles II told his brother, James, that he could have control of New Netherland. James, who was the duke of York, sent warships and soldiers to New Amsterdam. Stuyvesant wanted to defend New Amsterdam, but colonists were unhappy with his rule and refused to fight. The English promised the Dutch they could continue living their lives as they had been. However, the English threatened harsh punishment if the Dutch didn't **surrender**. New Netherland became an English colony, and it was renamed New York after the duke of York.

King Charles II

This picture shows New Netherland colonists begging Stuyvesant not to fight the incoming British soldiers.

The Royal Colony

New York was a **proprietary colony**. Most proprietary **charters** allowed colonies to have an elected **assembly**. James's charter didn't. This meant that colonists in New York didn't have a voice in their government.

In the beginning, James tried to be fair to the Dutch colonists. He allowed them to keep their land. James also continued to allow religious freedom. When he became King James II of England in 1685, New York's proprietary charter became a royal charter. That meant the king directly controlled the colony.

In 1688, the Catholic James II was removed from the throne and was replaced by a Protestant—King William III. One year later, New Yorkers **rebelled** against the colonial government. Jacob Leisler became the colonists' leader for almost two years. In 1691, the English ordered Leisler to step down, but he refused. The English government charged him with treason and hanged him.

King James II

12

William III and his wife, Mary, became king and queen of England after being offered the throne in an event called the "Glorious Revolution."

Unwanted Taxes

During the late 1700s, England passed laws and taxes without approval from colonial assemblies. This was against the colonies' charters. Colonists believed England only cared about the money it got from them, and that made them angry.

The colonists became even angrier after the French and Indian War (1754–1763), which was a series of wars in North America between England and France. England won, but the war cost it a lot of money. England wanted the colonies to help pay the cost. England also wanted the colonies to pay for soldiers to keep the peace between colonists and Native Americans. To raise money, King George III taxed the colonies on many goods—such as tea, sugar, and paper.

These laws and taxes raised the cost of goods and made it hard for merchants to carry on trade. In reply, colonists began to stage protests against England.

site of the Battle of Lake George during the French and Indian War

The Seige of Fort William Henry, shown here, occurred in 1757. The French took control of the New York fort to win a victory in the French and Indian War.

Protests in New York Colony

The colonists were angry about the new taxes and their lack of representation in English **Parliament**. The 1765 Stamp Act forced colonists to pay a tax on paper goods. Representatives from New York and other colonies held the Stamp Act Congress in New York City to protest. Some colonists **boycotted** English goods. England ended the tax in 1766 because the boycotts caused many problems.

The Quartering Act was another law that made New Yorkers angry. It said that colonists had to house, or quarter, English soldiers who were stationed in their cities. New Yorkers refused to do this. In return for New York's refusal, England took away their elected assembly's powers. Things became worse when England passed the **Coercive** Acts, which punished the colonies for their protests. Colonists called these acts the **Intolerable** Acts. New Yorkers began to feel they wouldn't be able to work out their problems with England. Many New York colonists joined people from the other English colonies to fight for freedom.

Stamp Act protestors in places such as New York City burned stamps to show their anger with England.

17

War Breaks Out

Not all the colonists were against English rule. Colonists called **loyalists** wanted to keep things the same in the colonies. Some colonists, called patriots, wanted the colonies to become independent of England. On September 5, 1774, members from 12 of the 13 colonies met in Philadelphia, Pennsylvania, for meetings that became known as the First Continental Congress. They gathered to discuss and protest the Coercive Acts and to boycott British goods. John Jay was one of eight New York representatives at the congress.

On April 19, 1775, battles between English soldiers and patriots took place in Lexington and Concord, Massachusetts. This marked the beginning of the American Revolution. One year later, on July 4, 1776, the Second Continental Congress approved the Declaration of Independence, which stated the 13 colonies were free from English rule. Jay was against war and didn't sign the declaration. However, once war started, he supported the colonies. Once New York approved the Declaration of Independence, the state quickly established its own government.

John Jay

General George Washington is shown here on his horse as the Declaration of Independence was read aloud in New York City on July 9, 1776.

New York Revolution!

New York was the stage for several key battles during the American Revolution. In the summer of 1776, English warships entered New York Harbor. The English beat the Continental army and occupied New York City for the rest of the war. While the English were there, fires broke out and destroyed about one-third of the city. Some people believed patriots were trying to burn English-occupied New York City to the ground.

The English won most of the battles during the first years of the war. The Americans needed help, but other countries didn't believe the colonists could win against rich and powerful England. In October 1777, the Americans finally won an important battle at Saratoga, New York. This made the French think the Americans could beat the English. France then sent troops and supplies to the colonies. In October 1781, General George Washington's Continental army defeated English troops at Yorktown, Virginia. The patriots had won the American Revolution.

This painting shows the surrender of the British at Saratoga on October 17, 1777.

Achieving Statehood

In September 1783, American and English officials signed the Treaty of Paris, which officially ended the American Revolution. New York City became the nation's temporary capital that year. In May 1787, representatives from the newly formed states met in Philadelphia to improve the national government. This meeting became known as the Constitutional Convention.

Alexander Hamilton, Robert Yates, and John Lansing Jr. represented New York at the convention. The members of the convention talked about different ideas for the government. Hamilton was in favor of a national government that was stronger than those of the states. This is what the United States has today. When the Constitution was written, Hamilton signed it. Yates and Lansing didn't, because they wanted stronger state governments. On July 26, 1788, New York became the 11th state to approve the Constitution. New York's colonial era had come to an end.

Glossary

assembly: A group of people who make and change laws for a government.

boycott: The act of refusing goods and services from a person or business in order to force change.

charter: A written statement describing the rights and responsibilities of a government and its citizens.

coercive: Using force to make people do things against their will.

intolerable: Something that is considered bad and won't be accepted.

loyalist: A colonist living in the English colonies who wanted the English to govern them.

New World: A term Europeans used for the Americas.

parliament: A lawmaking body, or legislature. Also, the name of the United Kingdom's legislative branch, which includes the House of Commons and House of Lords.

patroon: A person who received land in the New World from the Dutch government and hired settlers to farm it.

proprietary colony: Land given to someone so they can supervise how it is settled and developed.

rebel: To fight to overthrow a government.

surrender: To give up.

Index

Primary Source List

p. 9. *The Duke's Plan of New York: A Description of the Towne of Mannados or New Amsterdam as It Was in September 1661.* Creator unknown. Parchment. 1664. Based on map created by Jacques Cortelyou in 1661. Now kept at the British Library, London, UK.

p. 12. Portrait of King James II. From the workshop of Godfrey Kneller. Oil on canvas. 1680s. Current location unknown.

p. 13. *William III Landing at Brixham, Torbay, 5 November 1688.* Created by Jan Wyck. Oil on canvas. 1688. Now kept at the National Maritime Museum, Greenwich, London, UK.

p. 14. *View of the Lines at Lake George.* Created by Thomas Davies. Oil on canvas. 1774. Now kept at Fort Ticonderoga, New York.

p. 19 (inset). Portrait of John Jay. Created by Gilbert Stuart. Oil on canvas. 1794. Now kept at the National Gallery of Art, Washington, D.C.

Websites

Due to the changing nature of Internet links, PowerKids Press has developed an online list of websites related to the subject of this book. This site is updated regularly. Please use this link to access the list: www.powerkidslinks.com/s13c/ny